Walks from Your C

Coniston and Hawkshead

by
Tom Bowker

Dalesman Books
1990

Key to Maps

a summit

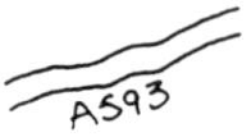

a road or walled lane

a tarn and beck

a lake

woodland

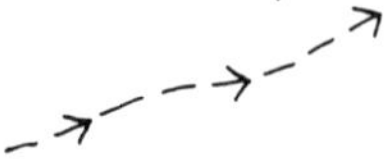

a footpath with direction arrow

a building

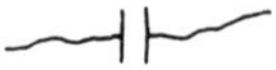

a bridge

a wall or fence that is particularly useful for navigation

cairns, caves, natural landmarks and points of interest

crag, quarry, precipitous slope

Contents

		Page
INTRODUCTION		4
FELL WALKS		
Walk 1.	Coniston Old Man and Dow Crag	6
Walk 2.	Tilberthwaite Gill, Wetherlam and Greenburn Tarn	9
Walk 3.	Swirl How, Great Carrs and Grey Friar	11
Walk 4.	Caw, White Maiden and Walna Scar	13
MEDIUM WALKS		
Walk 5.	Black Crag, Mountain Road, Tarn Hows and Tom Heights	17
Walk 6.	Hodge Close Quarries, Ivy Crag and Holme Fell	20
Walk 7.	The Yewdale Fells	22
Walk 8.	High Man and Lawson Park	24
Walk 9.	Beacon and Beacon Tarn	27
Walk 10.	The Park	30
Walk 11.	Claife Heights	32
Walk 12.	A Grizedale Forest Walk	35
Walk 13.	Goosey Foot Tarn and Hawkshead Moor	37
VALLEY WALKS		
Walk 14.	Coniston Lakeshore, Torver and Walna Scar	40
Walk 15.	Blelham Tarn, Windermere and Latterbarrow	43
Walk 16.	Boulder Valley and Levers Water	46

Cover design by Susan Smith.
Maps by Helen Bowker.

The Dalesman Publishing Company Ltd.,
Clapham, via Lancaster, LA2 8EB

First published 1984
Third edition 1990

ISBN: 0 85206 995 2

Printed by Peter Fretwell & Sons Ltd., Keighley, West Yorkshire BD21 1PZ

Introduction

THIS guidebook is not for the motorist who is looking for a couple of miles stroll in his driving shoes. Nor is it for the hardened fell-walker. It is written principally for the motorist-cum-walker who is prepared to pull on a pair of boots or stout walking shoes, sling a small pack on his back, and be happy to be out for at least two to three hours, or more. Many of the walks described will also appeal to family parties; to those introducing their children to the hills. For there are many facets to these walks other than the attaining of summits. There are tarns and pools for bathing, woods, waterfalls, caves and lovely picnic spots, all of which would appeal to children of all ages. All the walks are circular, starting and finishing at the same point but returning by a different route to that embarked upon in order to add interest. The walks described are roughly divided into three types.

1. **Valley Walks.** Genuine valley walks are at a premium in Lakeland. This is basically because the nearer to the valley floor the more problems with access over private or farm land, and that the very nature of the terrain eventually forces the walker uphill to some degree. None of the three described are genuine valley walks but they are the closest to this description of the sixteen. Given dry conditions, all these walks could be done in training shoes but it must be remembered that any Lakeland walk will have its boggy patches, and special care must be taken on the wet or slimy rocks at the edges of streams or waterfalls.

2. **Medium Walks.** These are walks that reach summits that are under two thousand feet in height. They form the bulk of the walks in the booklet for I felt they would appeal most to the kind of motorist-cum-walker-cum-family party described above. They often, however, cover similar terrain to the fell walks of Section 3 and strictly speaking the same rules about clothing and footgear described in that section apply here. Given dry summer conditions, most of these walks could be done in 'trainers' and in wet conditions 'wellies' would be an asset, but care must be taken on wet rock or at the edges of streams and waterfalls and stout walking shoes or boots are recommended.

3. **Fell Walks.** These are walks that reach one or more summits over two thousand feet in height. They are not however strenuous walks of their type, either being of no great length or over relatively easy ground, or both. Where there is any possibility of the walker getting into difficulty, easier alternatives are given. Nevertheless these are fell walks and should be treated with respect, especially in bad or winter conditions. I do not wish to labour the point but would not rest

easy if I did not enumerate here a few basic rules. It is advisable to wear boots, carry a map, compass, whistle and waterproofs. In winter a torch, gloves, balaclava, spare sweater, a plastic survival-bag and spare food are advisable additions. Loose-fitting jeans are okay in summer but warmer covering is advisable in winter. Never be afraid to turn back if the weather deteriorates. If you are forced to use your compass, start using it at a point where you know where you are, then you have a fixed point to return to; don't wait until you are lost!

All the walks described are accompanied by a rough sketch-map which used in combination with the text should prove adequate given good weather. It is advised, however, particularly for the fell-walks, to also carry the one-inch O.S. Lake District 'Tourist' Map, or the applicable sheet of the O.S. The English lakes, 1:25000 Outdoor Leisure Maps. As well as being a better aid to navigation, being more detailed than the sketch-map, they also help you to identify the various peaks and lakes seen from a particular viewpoint. The mileages are approximate and 'left' or 'right' refers to an object as if facing it. A note on car-parks is included with every walk but this situation can be somewhat fluid. Local authorities have a habit of restricting parking areas and/or opening up new ones some distance away from those described. So please don't blame the author if a particular parking situation differs from the description; it is as accurate and up-to-date as I can make it.

All the walks described here are on official rights-of-way, permissive footpaths, or public access areas. Routes can, however, be legally changed from time to time by developments or road improvements, in which case there should be a signpost specifically indicating the alteration.

When I was first given the opportunity to write this series of 'Walks From Your Car' booklets, I had some doubts about the project as my interest had always been with the high fells. As the work progressed, however, I found myself discovering facets of Lakeland that I was unaware existed, despite over thirty years of fell-walking. I became fascinated by hills and footpaths that I must admit I had previously scorned. I only hope that the purchasers of this booklet discover as much pleasure from these walks as I have. The popularity of these booklets has left me little spare time for revision. Any footpath changes differing from the first edition, which I have seen or been informed of, are included in this edition. Should you come across others and would be prepared to inform me of the details, via the publishers, you will receive my grateful thanks and your postage costs. Happy walking!

Tom Bowker

Fell Walks

Walk 1 **Fell Walk, 6-7 miles**

Coniston Old Man and Dow Crag

This is a fine walk which reaches the summit of one of Lakeland's most popular peaks by a route which is slightly longer, but more interesting, than the 'tourist' route. It also crosses the summit of one of the major rock-climbing crags of Lakeland, giving the fellwalker a bird's-eye view of climbers in action. Unfortunately the early part of the walk is among the unsightly debris of industry, both ancient and modern. For those interested, however, it is an important part of the story of Lakeland and one cannot help but have admiration for man's skill, courage, and ingenuity in wresting riches from the obdurate rock.

Parking: Coniston village car park.

LEAVE the village by the lane running to the right of the Black Bull Hotel. After crossing a cattle-grid the surface deteriorates and soon the wall on the left falls back, giving good views down onto the cascades of Church Beck. Soon a fine bridge crossing the beck will be met and a footpath sign indicating Coniston Old Man that way. Ignore this and continue straight ahead, into Coppermines Valley. It is a drab place, its green flanks scarred and hacked and its floor piled with spoil heaps and ruined workings. We can however lift our eyes up to a superb skyline, seeing from left to right, Coniston Old Man, Brim Fell, Swirl How, and Wetherlam.

Eventually the path begins to climb, past the Youth Hostel on your right, and then an underground pumping-station on your left. Ahead you will see the fine cascades of Levers Water Beck; when the path begins to swing up to the right leave it and walk left to the footbridge at the foot of the falls. Cross this and turn right to climb up the obvious path slanting across the old spoil heaps that have spilled down from the grim portal of Simon's Nick above. This path gives a superb view of the falls if they are in spate and ends on the crest of the

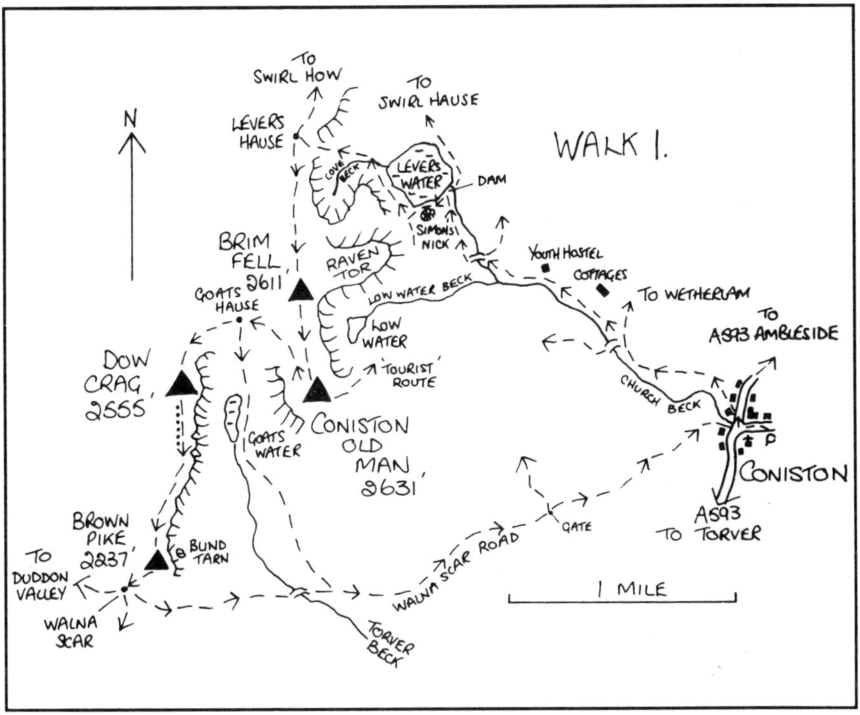

Levers Water Dam. The scars of industry are left behind now, the eye is soothed by graceful mountain shapes and the ear by the soft lap of water. The flat grassy top of the dam is a fine picnic or sun-bathing spot and the boulders of its facing make useful diving platforms.

The saddle at the head of the valley beyond the tarn is Swirl Hause, which divides the rugged mass of Wetherlam, on the right, from more shapely Swirl How, on the left. To the left of Swirl How is the saddle of Levers Hause, your next objective. To the extreme left the summit and cairn of the Old Man may be glimpsed. Looking back there is a fine view down onto Coniston Water and beyond, across the wooded hills of South Lakeland, to the distant Pennines, with the hump of Ingleborough predominant.

To continue walk along the crest of the dam, passing the fenced-off chasm of Simon's Nick, reputedly a thousand feet deep. This is the most horrendous of the many shafts, tunnels, and quarries riddling these fells. They are interesting but they are dangerous, please be careful. Beyond the dam a path bears right, across boulders and scree, above the tarn and below the steep rocks of Gill Cove Crags. Follow this until Cove Beck is crossed when it turns steeply left and uphill.

It is well cairned and eventually the angle eases as it climbs into Gill Cove but it steepens again for the final pull up to Levers Hause.

The tarn seen beyond the saddle is Seathwaite Tarn, above the Duddon Valley, beyond which rises the shapely peak of Harter Fell. Turn left here and follow the well-worn path along the broad ridge, bearing slightly east of south, to reach the summit cairn of Brim Fell. It is an easy walk now along to the summit of Coniston Old Man. There is a fine view down to your left into the blue depths of Low Water whilst over to your right the spiked summit of Dow Crag thrusts into view. A dip in the ridge reveals the great crag with the blue dot of the Mountain Rescue Box at its foot giving some idea of scale. If a wish to return to Coniston is felt, from the summit of the Old Man, simply follow the eroded 'tourist' route leading down past Low Water and through the old quarries to meet the Walna Scar road and so back to Coniston village.

For those who wish to continue, and the interest is certainly worth the extra expenditure of energy, retrace your steps for a short way until you see a path bearing away to your left. This slants down across steepening grassy slopes, above the dark waters of Goat's Water, to reach the broad grassy saddle of Goats Hause. For those who wish it the walk can be shortened here by turning left down to the tarn, where a fine path along its eastern shore eventually leads on down to the Walna Scar track. To continue, however, follow the path swinging and climbing steeply left to reach the massive blocks that form the summit of Dow Crag. To the north-west the Scafells look particularly fine and to their left, on a clear day, the Isle of Man may be spotted.

Continue along the ridge, alongside an old wall at first, to reach the head of Great Gully. A circumspect peek over the edge gives some idea of the scale of the crag. Further down the ridge, from the rim of Easy Gully, a safer bird's-eye view may possibly be had of 'crag-rats' in action. The ridge climbs again to reach the summit of Brown Pike. Down to the left may be seen the tiny Blind Tarn, so-called because it has no outlet stream. From Brown Pike a worn grassy path leads down to the crest of Walna Scar Pass. Turn left here and follow the worn track back to Coniston village. On your way you will get magnificent views of Dow Crag to your left, with the dark rift of Great Gully predominant.

Tilberthwaite Gill, Wetherlam and Greenburn Tarn

Not for the inexperienced in mist, or hard winter conditions, but under clear skies a delightful mountain walk. The views are superb and for those interested there are many fascinating aspects of the industrial history of Lakeland.

Parking: About a mile and a half north of Coniston Village, on the A593 Coniston to Ambleside road, there is a minor road branching left signposted 'Tilberthwaite, No Through Road'. Follow this road until just before a bridge an open area will be seen on the left, below spoil heaps. Park here (GR:306009).

A PATH, signposted 'Tilberthwaite Gill', will be seen climbing up through the slate; follow this. As you climb you will pass openings into the quarry on your left. Go into the third (or it could be fourth) one which leads you into the upper level of the quarry and gives superb views down into the lower levels and across low wooded hills to distant Fairfield and its companion fells. Return to the path and follow it until it forks. Take the right fork which leads down into the bed of the gill, passing a seat, to a footbridge. Cross the bridge and turn left following the path along the bank of the gill. When the gill begins to swing right, scramble up rocks to another footbridge at the base of the gorge. This bridge is for viewing purposes only. The section of Tilberthwaite Gill above this bridge was a major tourist attraction around the turn of the century with a network of bridges and walkways. These were allowed to fall into disrepair, however, and beyond the viewing bridge is now only for those with some rock-climbing experience.

Return from the bridge a short way then turn left to climb steeply up to a stile in a fence. Slightly easier going then brings you to a broad path; turn left along this. Soon there is a dramatic drop into the gill on your left and care must be taken if the path is icy. The view ahead is dominated by the towering bulk of Wetherlam. When the path forks go left down to and across a footbridge over a beck. Above and beyond the bridge an obvious ridge (Steel Edge), clearly identifiable by two man-made rifts at its foot, thrusts out from the main mass of Wetherlam. These are filled-in mine entrances and if you glance upstream you will see the ruined workings of the Tilberthwaite Copper Mine. Climb past the openings and steeply up to reach the crest of a well-

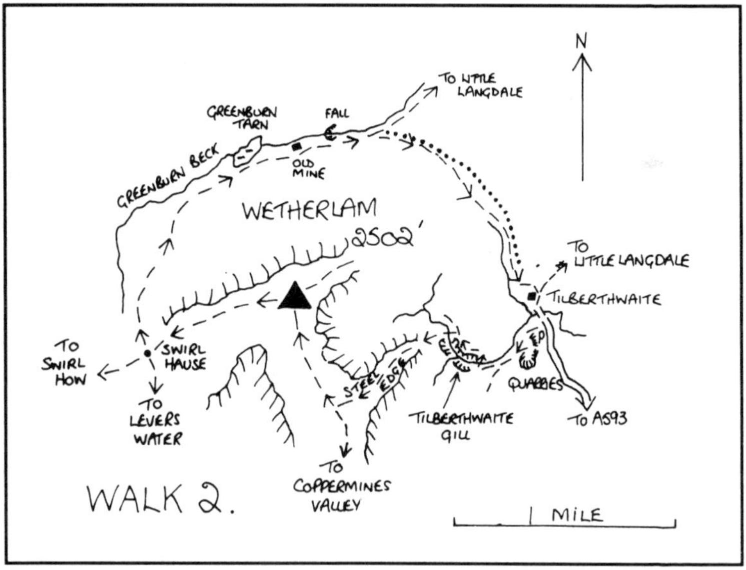

defined ridge. This leads to a steeper rockier section followed by grass which eases back onto the broad summit ridge of Wetherlam near a tiny tarn. Walk to the right of the tarn to shortly join a well-worn path. Turn right, along this. The valley to your left now is Red Dell and beyond it rise Coniston Old Man and Swirl How. Behind you there is an even more extensive view of Coniston Water. The path leads easily to the summit and just before reaching it there is a bird's-eye view down a gully to your right.

The view from the summit is superb, ranging from the distant hump of Ingleborough to the south-east to the rugged massif of the Scafells in the north-west. It is an ideal place to take out your map and try to orientate yourself. For the descent follow the path heading W to WSW, which runs around the rim of the escarpment, with the drop on your right, before dropping down to the saddle and cairn of Swirl Hause.

The rocky ridge rising beyond the saddle leads up to Swirl How (Walk 3). You however turn right at the saddle, down into Greenburn. The craggy peak to your left, as you descend, is Great Carrs and a careful look at the scree below it may reveal the aircraft wreckage described in Walk 3. The path down Greenburn is indistinct but after passing a huge and obvious boulder just head down towards Greenburn Beck which leads down to Greenburn Tarn. This tarn was dammed in 1812 to provide a source of power for the Greenburn Copper Mine. Follow the path across the dam, admiring its solid construction and the hardiness of the men who built it. Beyond this, boggy ground leads down to the ruined mine-buildings. Up to your right you will see a well-preserved 'sledgate' zig-zagging down the fellside. Ore was brought down to the smelter on sledges, hence the name.

A good path leaves the buildings and heads down the valley. Follow this path, with a detour to the left to view a fine waterfall, down to a gate in a wall. Do not go through the gate, turn right and follow the wall uphill. The wall crosses a crest into a dip then climbs steeply again, where, beyond a stile, it veers sharply left. Leave the wall at this point and bear right to a stile in a fence. Cross the stile and go down a valley towards the head of an obvious deep-cut gill, the wall coming back towards you on the left. At the head of the gill ignore the gate in the wall and follow the path running down between the wall and the gill. This drops away steeply and soon there is a fine view down onto Tilberthwaite and your car. Follow the path down to the rear of some cottages to find a gate which leads you around the front of them and so to the road.

Walk 3 **Fell Walk, 6-7 miles**

Swirl How, Great Carrs and Grey Friar

A fine walk over three of the less well-known, but in no way inferior, of the Coniston Fells. The approach, like many in the area, passes through scenes of industrial history to reach scenes of rugged mountain beauty. Once upon the ridges there is easy high-level walking giving superb all-round views.

Parking: Coniston village car park.

FOLLOW the directions given in Walk 1 as far as Levers Hause or, if you have already completed Walk 1 and feel like change of approach, turn to Walk 16. Follow the directions given here as far as Levers Water, then continue with Walk 1 to reach Levers Hause. Upon reaching Levers Hause turn right and follow the ridge, first north-east then north, over the subsidiary tops of Little and Great How Crags to reach the summit cairn of Swirl How. If there is cloud about and you are

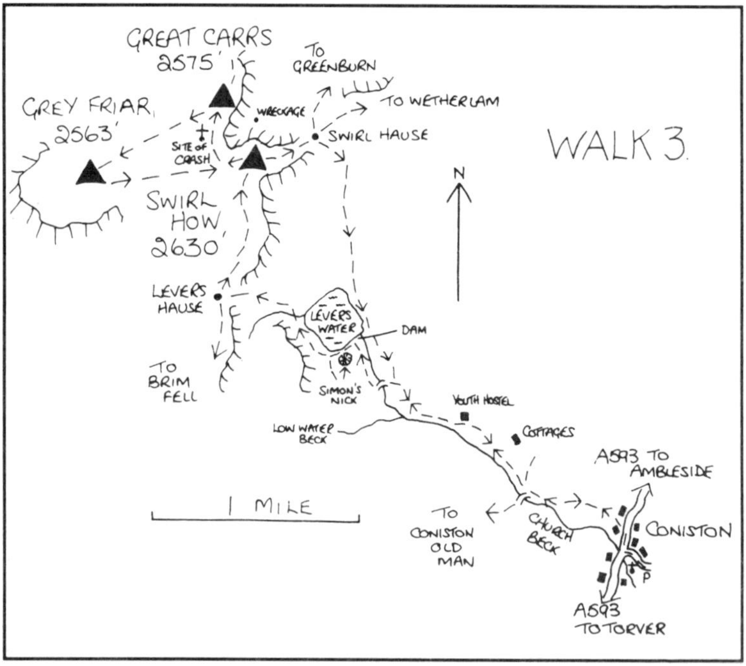

in doubt the summit cairn is the furthest one, perched on the very edge where the steep east flank swings west.

The tarn in the valley immediately below is Greenburn Tarn and beyond it lies Little Langdale. The neighbouring fell to the east is Wetherlam and to the left and beyond this the fells swing round in a great arc from shapely Ill Bell, above Troutbeck, to the rugged Scafells, beyond the craggy summit of Great Carrs, your next objective. To reach Great Carrs descend westerly (left) before swinging north around the grassy rim of Broad Slack. Peer over the rim to spot the wreckage of a Halifax bomber that struck the summit ridge of Great Carrs whilst returning from a bombing raid over Europe and disintegrated, with the loss of its crew. As you climb up to the summit of Great Carrs, move left to spot a wooden cross set above piled wreckage on a patch of still scorched earth marking the scene of impact. Framed against the majestic backcloth of the Scafells, it makes a dramatic and moving picture. From Great Carrs you can look down upon the shining beetles toiling painfully up the zig-zags of Hardknott Pass, whilst to the south the dome of Coniston Old Man contrasts strongly with the steepled top of Dow Crag.

From here a path leads easily, and south-westerly, down into a dip and then up to the summit of Grey Friar, probably the most infrequently climbed of all the Coniston high fells. From here there is a fine view down the Duddon Valley towards Black Combe, to your left, whilst, to your right, the eye is led up Mosedale and into the rugged heart of Upper Eskdale and the magnificent horsehoe of Crinkle Crags, Bowfell, Esk Pike and the Scafells. Return to Swirl How either by way of Great Carrs or by heading directly to it. From Swirl How follow the curiously-named Prison Band ridge heading E to NE and down to the saddle of Swirl Hause, with fine views down to your right to Levers Water and Coniston Water beyond.

Upon reaching Swirl Hause turn right and follow the good path which leads down to Levers Water and eventually the dam. From here either follow the Land Rover track down the left-hand bank of Levers Water Beck, or cross the outflow from the dam and follow the more interesting path down the right bank across the spoil heaps of Simon's Nick. Both ways meet at the foot of Levers Water Beck and from there follow the Coppermines Valley road back to Coniston village.

Walk 4 **Fell Walk, 8-9 miles**

Caw, White Maiden and Walna Scar

This is a delightful fell-walk for those who seek less well-trodden summits. For the inexperienced walker it is best left for a clear day, for these modest heights are surprisingly craggy and lack the usual network of well-worn paths. The views are very fine for the walk passes through a pleasing variety of scenery.

Parking: From Torver follow the A593 towards Broughton-in-Furness. Around a mile from Torver turn right up a steep minor road. Continue past a quarry road entrance and alongside plantations to a car-park and picnic site in the trees to your right. (GR:253927).

CROSS the fence by a stile and follow a path which at present descends down the edge of a felled area to debouch on to a forest road. Turn left to a junction. Turn right and follow a forest road over and down to where a stony path slants sharply down to your left. Follow this down to and across a concrete bridge over the Appletree Worth Beck. Continue uphill past a shed to emerge on to another forest road. Turn left and follow this road to where a blue-waymarked path forks right into the trees. Turn right and follow this undulating and twisting path, waymarked on the tree trunks by blue paint daubs, and passing close to an old wall at one point, to eventually descend and emerge onto a forest road. Turn right to shortly see a path veering down to your left. Follow this, passing an old shed, to a gate leading on to a tarmac road. Turn right and follow the road to cross the River Lickle over humpbacked Water Yeat Bridge. Continue up the road towards Stephenson Ground Farm. Caw, crowned by its man-like cairn, offers a shapely challenge ahead. More distantly to your right White Pike thrusts a surprisingly rugged profile above the headwaters of the Lickle.

Beyond the first building at Stephenson Ground follow a 'Walna Scar' sign through a gate on your right then turn left behind the farm buildings to climb a grassy path alongside a wall. This eventually climbs between walls to a gate leading on to the open fellside. Follow a path rightwards for a short way to where a faint path veers left into a boggy gap. This path heads virtually directly, but intermittently, towards the summit of Caw, roughly following the upper reaches of Broadslack Beck towards the trig point. The final slope is steep and rocky but the extensive view is worth all your efforts. Now head north-easterly, down then up, along an intermittent path, to 'bag' the lower, rocky, plurally and prosaically-named Pikes. Beyond the next dip White Pike throws up surprisingly steep and craggy defences for a fell that from most angles looks like a dull grassy spur. Beyond rises eroded-path slashed Brown Pike with the spiky summit of Dow Crag to its left. Between them looms the old bald dome of Coniston Old Man. Left of Dow Crag rise Swirl How and Great Carrs with Grey Friar yet further left. Beyond Grey Friar the Scafells throw massive shadows into the bowl of Upper Eskdale. Across the Duddon Valley rises solitary but shapely Harter Fell.

Now head down into the dip below to join the bridleway linking Stephenson Ground with Walna Scar. Turn left in the dip and follow the bridleway around to the disused Walna Scar Quarry. The path is indistinct at first but improves into a built-up track as it curves around the fellside. Walna Scar Quarry is extensive and if you explore upwards a high narrow fissure leads you into a huge man-made pit where a 'gurt' cavern gapes evilly in a corner. I once stepped out of the rift to come face to face with a handsome fox. The dog/vixen appeared unperturbed and drifted lazily but lissomly up the steep spoil, pausing frequently to give me an interrogative stare, before vanishing amongst some piled boulders.

Retreat back through the fissure and climb right, around the rim of the pit, before slanting right up steep grass to emerge close to the cairn crowning White Pike. Now head east-north-east into a dip where a wall climbs up from the right and follow this wall to reach the summit cairn of White Maiden and enjoy a sudden view of Coniston Water. The wall turns down to the right here, providing a good escape route should bad weather or fatigue assault you. Now head north-east along a broad undulating ridge to reach the small cairn crowning

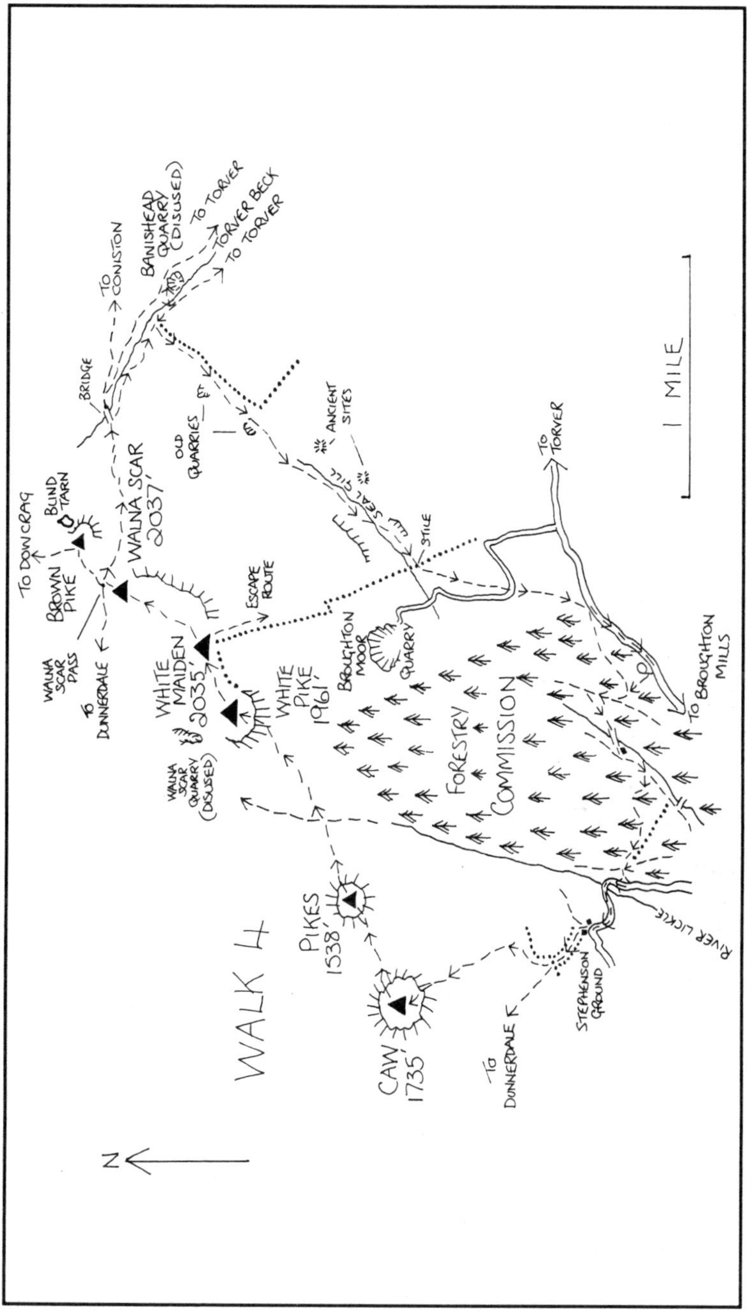

WALK 4
N
CAW
1735'
PIKES
1538'
WHITE
PIKE
1961'
WHITE
MAIDEN
2035'
WALNA SCAR
2037'
BROWN
PIKE
BLIND
TARN
TO DOW CRAG
WALNA
SCAR
PASS
TO
DUNNERDALE
ESCAPE
ROUTE
WALNA
SCAR
QUARRY
(DISUSED)
BROUGHTON
MOOR
QUARRY
FORESTRY
COMMISSION
TO BROUGHTON
MILLS
RIVER LICKLE
STEPHENSON
GROUND
TO
DUNNERDALE
STILE
SEAL GILL
TO
TORVER
ANCIENT
SITES
OLD
QUARRIES
BRIDGE
TO
CONISTON
BANISHEAD
QUARRY
(DISUSED)
TO TORVER
TORVER BECK
TO TORVER
1 MILE

Walna Scar, overlooking the better-known pass of that name.

Drop down into the dip and turn right down the worn and stony track. Lower down you may spot a small stone edifice on your left that was reputedly a shelter for folk overtaken by fatigue or bad weather in the days when this was a vital trade and travellers' highway. Continue down to the iron-railed stone bridge over the Torver Beck. From here look up into the great corrie behind Coniston Old Man dominated by the baroque and darkly-cloven splendour of Dow Crag. Do not cross the bridge. Turn down the path along the right bank of Torver Beck. Just before this path passes through a gap in a wall near a sheepfold turn right along a faint path along the foot of the slope, some yards from the wall but running parallel to it. Soon this path improves and the view ahead opens up to reveal the ruined workshops of Ash Gill Quarry. Beyond these the skyline dips between rounded Bleaberry Haws and a rugged ridge rising up to White Maiden. This far dip is your objective. The wall on your left turns away on approaching the ruins. You pass through them to cross Ash Gill Beck below a waterfall. Now head up either bank of Seal Gill towards the dip. Path traces are faint and intermittent. Small cairns and hollows on the left bank are dignified as 'sites of antiquity' on the 2 1/2" map. Must have been a bit 'parky' up here with only woad long-johns between you and the Helm Wind!

Go through the dip and down to where an obvious grassy ramp climbs up on to the left bank. Follow this down to find a stone stile in a wall. This wall is the 'escape route' from White Maiden previously mentioned. Cross the stile and walk down to join a tarmac strip serving the unsightly collection of sheds nestling in a raw gaping wound of slate that is the working Broughton Mill Quarry. Turn left up the tarmac. When it curves left, near some posts, leave it and head right, across the moor, towards the corner of woods. Beyond a boggy dip a built-up path leads up to a stile near the corner of the wood. Cross it and turn right up the road to your car.

Medium Walks

Walk 5 **Medium Walk, 5-6 miles**

Black Crag, Mountain Road, Tarn Hows and Tom Heights

A walk spiced with a variety of scenery and terrain. Should be reserved for a fine day because the all-round views are very fine. Nowhere strenuous though occasionally boggy. Ideal for a family party because the Tarn Hows and Tom Heights section could be left for another day should some members of the party tire and a return made down the Mountain Road, which would still give an enjoyable but curtailed walk.

Parking: From Coniston take the A593 Ambleside road for about three and a half miles, beyond the highest point, to a forked minor road branching left signposted 'High Park/Oxen Fell (Unfit for Cars?), also marked 'Cumbria Way' on 2 1/2" SW map. Park on verges. (GR:329022)

CROSS the main road and go up the track opposite, passing a seat. Go through a gate and follow the path which runs alongside a wall. This leads down to a stream and a boggy area. This can be avoided by moving higher up the slope to where the path can be faintly seen zig-zagging up the hill. The wall too has swung right and is still to your left. Turn around here for a splendid view, with Harrison Stickle and the great crag of Pavey Ark predominant to your left front and the more prosaic shapes of Helvellyn and Fairfield to your right.

The path approaches the wall near two gates. Go through the upper gate and turn right alongside the wall. The path is indistinct here but if you veer left you will meet a more obvious path coming in from your left. Turn right along this and follow it towards Low Arnside farm, seen ahead. Go through a gateway, boggy, and follow a more distinct and stony path bearing away to your left. There is a fine view of Wetherlam to your right beyond the farm buildings. The path twists and turns across open ground before passing through a gateway to run alongside a wall, on your right. Beyond a further gate the ground levels and a large bog can be seen to your left. Turn left just before the bog to follow a faint path leading left around a rocky knoll and across a wet patch to meet a built-up path which appears to be emerging from the bog. Turn left along this and follow it with a wall to your left. Eventually, when the path begins to descend, a small cairn will be seen on your right opposite a 'hog-hole' in the wall to your left. Turn right here and climb up the grass to the crest above. From here Black Crag will be seen, crowned by a distinctive square-cut cairn, beyond a boggy hollow. Skirt the hollow and scramble up to the cairn.

The views are superb, that of Windermere being particularly dramatic as you step up to the cairn. Blelham Tarn is nearer below and to the right of that and above Hawkshead is Esthwaite Water. To the right of Hawkshead there is a glimpse of Tarn Hows and beyond that the gleaming length of Coniston Water, with the waters of distant Morecambe Bay further beyond. Coniston Old Man rises to the right of the lake followed by the lower but more dominant, from this angle, Wetherlam. The knobbles of Crinkle Crags lead to Bowfell, with the pointed and nearer peak of Pike O'Blisco below them. The Langdale Pikes are obvious, followed by the more prosaic shapes of High Raise and Ullscarf leading to Steel Fell and the gap of Dunmail Raise. On a particularly clear day Blencathra might be seen rising above this dip. Helvellyn, Seat Sandal, the Fairfield peaks and Red Screes lead to the gap of Kirkstone Pass, followed by High Street and the shapely duo of Froswick and Ill Bell. Beyond them are the distant Pennines with the hump of Ingleborough predominant.

For the descent retrace your footsteps to a cairn which is the start of a cairned path running beside a little pool and in the general direction of Tarn Hows. The path is well-marked and continues over open ground eventually to meet the original path beyond the large bog. Turn left here and follow the path down through woods to reach the Mountain Road. Turn right along this. Glimpses of Tarn Hows will be seen through the trees to your left. After a steep drop left a gate will be seen marked 'The Tarns'. If you wish to curtail the walk at this point continue down the Mountain Road until it meets the main road. Cross this and enter the lane opposite. Then turn immediately right and walk through trees to cross a footbridge to reach a stile beyond. Cross the stile and follow the wall to a further stile. Cross this and you are back at your car.

If you wish to continue, however, turn left through the gate. Notice a faint path coming down on your right. This will be your return route. Upon approaching the tarn take the left-hand path, crossing the beck by a footbridge. A well-worn path now leads around the tarn. When it forks take the lower branch which gives lovely views of the tree-clad island and promontories. Curve round the southern end of the tarn to reach a small dam. Cross the dam and just beyond it take the path climbing up through the trees on your left. A short climb brings the first of a series of rocky knolls giving superb views. Continue over these to the furthest and highest cairn. Move left here to find yourself on the lip of a huge amphitheatre. Coniston Water is to your left and below you are the dark waters of Yew Tree Tarn. Beyond rises the

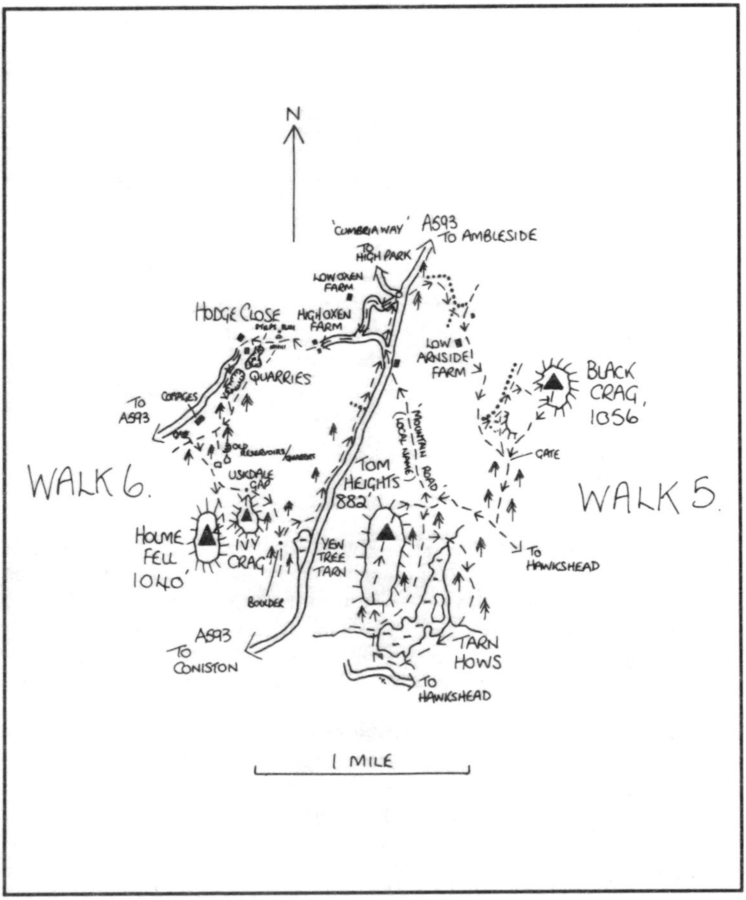

rugged height of Holme Fell and beyond that Coniston Old Man and Wetherlam. To the right of Wetherlam, Crinkle Crags and Bowfell, divided by Pike O'Blisco, are impressive from this angle. The fells beyond them are largely as described from Black Crag, which can be seen half right ahead.

For the descent continue with the path along the ridge which passes to the left of a small pool. Soon the Mountain Road will be seen below to your right. The path winds towards it to meet it at the entrance gate. Follow the 'road' to reach your car as previously described.

Hodge Close Quarries, Ivy Crag and Holme Fell

This superb short walk has infinite variety packed into its few miles. Hodge Close quarries may be a massive industrial scar but they are an integral part of Lakeland history. They have a dramatic beauty peculiarly their own and have become the playground of Lakeland's young 'tigers'. Holme Fell must be one of the most rugged of Lakeland's lower fells. The summit has a high-mountain feeling and the view from it is very fine.

Parking: As for Walk 5.

TAKE the left-hand fork of the minor road, past Low Oxen Farm, to a road junction. Turn right here to reach High Oxen Farm (note the date 1673 over the door). Go through the farmyard and through a gate leading on to a muddy track. After dropping into a hollow and crossing a beck the track climbs, twists and undulates whilst offering fine views. It eventually drops towards the buildings of Hodge Close, passing between a gate in a fence on your left and a small reedy tarn, with a ruin beyond, on your right. Shortly beyond these and before reaching the main buildings look for a narrow flight of slate steps leading down to your left. Descend these and the path through piled boulders below on to the floor of a huge quarry. Continue under a massive rock archway on to a rusting platform projecting over the deep green water flooding an even more spectacular quarry. Climbers may be in action on the vertiginous rocks to your left and if you are unfortunate 'frogmen/women' may have stirred the translucent depths into a milky broth a-bobbing with varied litter.

Retrace your steps and upon emerging from the slate stairway turn left then left again to pass a cottage. Shortly you will emerge on to the dizzy rim of the flooded quarry. Continue around the rim to a gate. You will notice that the further depths of the quarry have been used by generations of Lakeland folk as a dumping ground for 'clapped-out jalopies' and'owd baths'. Go through the gate to join and follow a path climbing gently rightwards through woodland alongside a wall. Pass through a gate. Presently the woods over the wall end and a row of cottages may be seen. Just before reaching a further gate look for a path climbing left. Follow this to a grassy crest from which you look over a heathery hollow to a rugged skyline. The prominent cairn marks the summit of Ivy Crag, with the higher summit of Holme Fell to its right. The gap below and to the left of Ivy Crag is Uskdale Gap. Bear right across the hollow to find and climb a path through the heather up onto the summit of Holme Fell which lies at the far end of a pronounced ridge. From the cairn there is a superb view down the length of Coniston Water. To the right of Coniston Water, Coniston Old Man and nearer Wetherlam dominate the skyline. From Wetherlam around to Black Crag (Walk 5) there is a splendour of mountains — Crinkle Crags, Pike O'Blisco, Bowfell, Glaramara, the Langdale Pikes, Pavey Ark, High Raise, the gap of Dunmail Raise, Helvellyn and Fairfield. Return along the summit ridge before dropping right and heading towards Ivy Crag. From its cairn the all-round view is equally spectacular. Yew Tree Tarn lies immediately below in the wooded depths of Yewdale, across which Tom Heights guards the popular and lovely Tarn Hows.

Head north from Ivy Crag and down into the Uskdale Gap. Turn right here and descend a steepish loose path towards Yew Tree Tarn. When a prominent boulder is reached turn left and follow a faint path to meet a wall coming in from your right. Turn left alongside the wall or pass through a gap in the wall and walk in the space between the wall and woodland. Either way leads to a stile. Cross the stile to follow a path veering left to a gate leading on to the A593, signposted 'Holme Fell'. Ignore the gate and follow a faint path leftwards, climbing the fellside alongside the road and its bordering wall. At the top of the hill a stile leads on to the road. Ignore it and continue alongside the wall/road. Climb a stile over a crossing wall and a further stile leading on to a minor road signposted 'High Oxen Farm'. Cross this, walk through trees and over a footbridge to cross a stile into a field. Continue alongside the wall to a stile which leads you back on to the road close to your car.

The Yewdale Fells

This walk has a high-mountain flavour largely because of the rugged scenery it passes through. It is nowhere strenuous and is a good introductory walk for children before they attempt the higher fells. It can be done equally as well from Coniston as from Tilberthwaite but I personally feel it is more interesting starting and finishing in Tilberthwaite.

Parking: As for Walk 2.

FOLLOW the directions given in Walk 2 as far as where the path forks right down into the gill. Take the left fork here which climbs high above the left bank of the gill, giving interesting views down into it. The path gradually swings to the right, above the gill, passing an old mine shaft. There is a fine view here of the craggy face of Wetherlam towering above. The ridge (Steel Edge), taken by Walk 2 can be seen to advantage from here. Look along the base of Wetherlam and pick out the various mine shafts.

The path begins to swing left and forks, the right-hand branch crossing a stream. Ignore this and continue with the original path which keeps swinging left. If you look ahead you will see the continuation of your path climbing up the valley towards a gap in the skyline. After crossing above a fine rocky cascade the path becomes an obviously constructed one and quarried openings are seen in the fellside to your left. The path was once used for mining or quarrying purposes. As you approach the gap ahead it begins to frame the shapely summit of Coniston Old Man. Before reaching the gap look for a cairn on your right and a path climbing towards Wetherlam. At this point it is worth detouring left up the grass slope and then across to the obvious cairn on the skyline. This is Kitty Crag, the highest point of the Yewdale Fells, from where a superb view of Coniston Water is seen. The despoiled Coppermines Valley, with its ruined workings and white-washed Youth Hostel, lies below to your right. Above and beyond are, from left to right, Coniston Old Man, Brim Fell, Swirl How, and near at hand, Wetherlam. Below Coniston Old Man can be seen Low Water and below Swirl How a section of Levers Water. Behind Wetherlam can be seen the old mine-workings at the entrance to Red Dell.

Return to the path and continue up to the gap. From here follow a zig-zag path, probably an old 'sledgate' by which slate or ore was dragged down the valley on sledges, to reach the valley floor just to

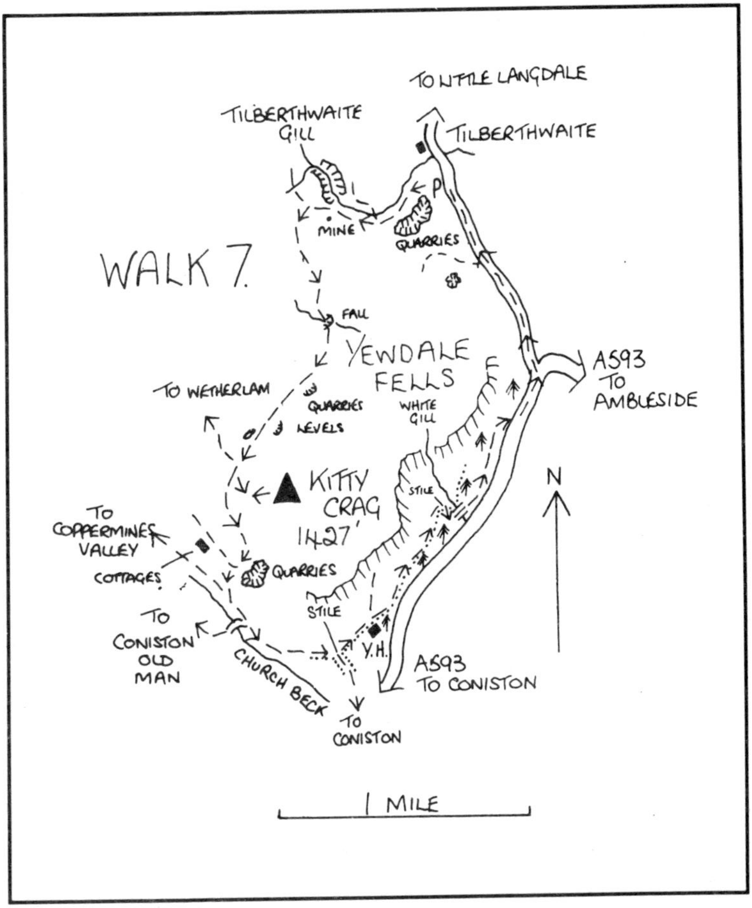

the left of a row of old miners' cottages, now presumably holiday cottages. Turn left here and follow the rough road down towards Coniston alongside and above the fine cascades of Church Beck. Just beyond and below a cattle-grid and just before the track enters a walled lane, look for a stile to your left. Cross this and follow the path running alongside the wall to reach the rear of Coniston Youth Hostel. Hereabouts a path will be seen climbing up the fellside to your left. Ignore this, for although a footpath is clearly marked on the O.S. Maps leading across the Yewdale Fells to Tilberthwaite, the middle section is virtually non-existent and if you do not know the ground you can find yourself embarked upon a nasty descent into Tilberthwaite through thick juniper and steep crags.

Continue with the wall on your right. In wet weather this path is a bit boggy and there are a few low branches to watch out for. After crossing a stream you eventually reach the foot of a magnificent waterslide. Cross the stile over the wall to your right and follow an indistinct path running alongside the stream. When the ground starts to level out look for a gap in the wall across the other side of the stream. Cross the stream and go through the gap to find a more obvious path which leads to a stile at a junction of walls. Go over this and follow the path which now bears left to another stile. Cross this and follow the path through the woods with the road near at hand to your right. Eventually it emerges onto the road a short distance away from the turn-off to Tilberthwaite. Walk back along this road to reach your car.

Walk 8 **Medium Walk, 5-7 miles**

High Man and Lawson Park

This pleasant walk offers a wide variety of scenery. The best views are seen on the early and later sections of the walk. The middle section along the ridgeway of High Man is enclosed by forest but it has its own charm, despite being a little boggy in parts. All the climbing and road-walking is done in the first mile of the walk.

Parking: Park in the Monk Coniston car park situated on the eastern shore at the head of the lake. (GR:316978).

LEAVE the car park and turn to the right up the road. Within a few yards a footpath sign will be seen on the left; follow this. The path goes between a wall and fence before reaching a gate beyond a beck. Beyond the gate turn left and head up into the top corner of the field. A stile on the left is reached. Cross this, turn right, then left, and follow a path running alongside, and to the left, of a stream. When a house is reached, follow the diversion signs around the back of the house before returning to the original line. The path swings right, over a stream. Beyond the stream look for a gap in a fence on your left marked with a yellow way-marker. Go through the gap and continue up to meet and cross a stile leading onto a road.

Turn left up the road to a junction with another road near an ornamental fountain and horse-trough. Continue past the fountain until you see a gate on your right accompanied by a footpath sign. Go through the gate and follow the path which swings to the right to a gate. Go through the gate then turn immediately left up a stony path. The path begins to climb with a wall to its left. As height is gained a marvellous view opens up to your right and behind you. Across Coniston Water the Brown Pike to Dow Crag ridge disappears behind Coniston Old Man. From Coniston Old Man the skyline undulates over Swirl How and then Wetherlam. Beyond Wetherlam are the prominent shapes of the Langdale Pikes. Well to the right of these and rising above the wooded hills guarding Tarn Hows rise Helvellyn, Fairfield and Red Screes. On a very clear day Blencathra may be seen through the gap of Dunmail Raise to the left of Helvellyn.

As the path levels off the wall swings away left and after crossing a stream the path swings in the same direction. It is indistinct here so just head up towards the wall ahead in which two distinctive pointed stones can be picked out. These are old gateposts and beyond them a stile leads onto a forest road. Turn right along this and then almost immediately turn left onto another track leading into the woods. Follow this to a T-junction and turn right here. Soon another T-junction is reached. Cross the junction and go into the gap between the trees where a path follows the direction of power lines. Soon a tower will be seen rising ahead. The path heads towards this between the woods; it is an old right-of-way and you will notice it is marked by standing slates which are the remnants of an old fence. Another forest road is crossed before the tower is reached. When this is reached another fire tower is seen ahead. Head for this; it crowns High Man and is only occupied during times of great hazard.

After leaving the tower continue along the gap in the forest marked by the standing slates. Soon you will pass a hide built by the Manpower Services Commission. The path drops down to a boggy section to the right of a reedy moss. Beyond this it climbs and the woods close in. Shortly after passing through some ancient larches a forest road is met. Turn left along this to a junction of roads. Turn right here to shortly reach another junction. Turn right again. There is a sign indicating 'Lawson Park' here. The road rises to a brow and about one hundred yards beyond the brow a footpath will be seen leading into the woods on your right. Go down this.

It is wet in places and soon you will glimpse Dow Crag and Coniston

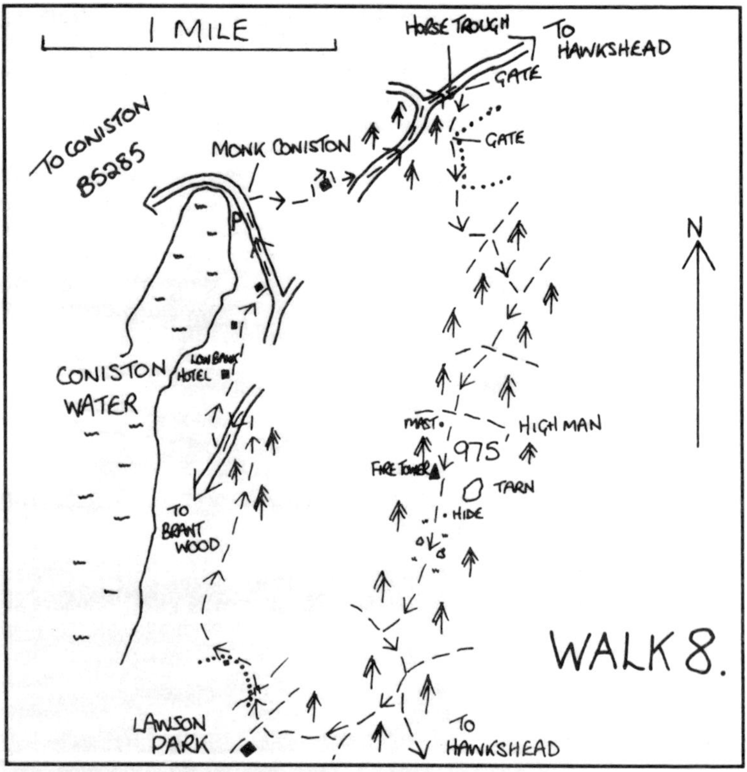

Old Man above the trees ahead. The path ends at a gateway leading onto a broader track. The building to the left is Lawson Park. There is a fine view from here across the lake. Cross the track and drop down the far bank and follow a footpath sign marked 'Coniston'. Pass through a gate. Beyond the fence to your left there is a superb view of the Coniston Fells. From left to right they are Dow Crag, Coniston Old Man, Brim Fell, Swirl How, Black Sails and Wetherlam. Immediately below Swirl How you look directly into the Coppermines Valley where the white-walled Youth Hostel can be seen. Go down through a gate and over a wooden bridge. The path then climbs alongside a wall. Ignore all diversions around here and continue past a barn on your left, with a fine view down the lake. Beacon is prominent at the foot of the lake and to its right Black Combe can be seen down the Torver Valley.

Continue with the path through woodland, ignoring a stile and yellow markers to your left. The path goes over a culvert and through a gate with two magnificent beeches rising over the wall to the left. Further gates and a footbridge lead down to a road. Turn left along the road for a short way until a stile and footpath sign are seen on the right. Cross the stile and follow the path slanting across a field to a slab over a stream and a kissing-gate in a wall. Beyond this the path swings right, then left, before passing through a gate in a fence to reach a kissing-gate which leads onto the drive of the *Low Bank Hotel.* Cross the drive to another kissing-gate and follow the path alongside the hotel drive to a stile and kissing-gate in a corner under a tree. Continue straight ahead, crossing a farm road, keeping a wall to your left. The wall ends where a narrow passage-way turns left, yellow way-marker on right wall. Go through passage, down steps, and follow a fence to reach a stile. There are decrepit buildings to your right. Beyond the stile follow the path contouring right to a stile on the left of a gate. This leads into a lane which runs up to a road. Turn left here and Monk Coniston car park is shortly reached.

Walk 9 **Medium Walk, 4 miles**

Beacon and Beacon Tarn

A mildly energetic walk to reach the summit of a shapely fell of modest height, and to visit the shores of a lovely tarn. The views from Beacon are delightful.

Parking: On the Torver Common car park which is situated about a mile south of Torver, on the A5084, on the left-hand side, part way down a steep hill, beyond a garage (GR:287927).

CROSS the road to a 'Public Footpath' sign and stile. Cross the stile and follow the path to the right to a footbridge over the Torver Beck. Go over the bridge and along the path climbing up through the bracken and into the valley ahead. You will be following a stream, Mere Beck, down to your left. When the valley begins to open out you will see the impressive shape of Beacon ahead. In order to climb it you must first reach the obvious gap in the skyline to the right of it. You will now see a path on the other side of Mere Beck. Eventually you will

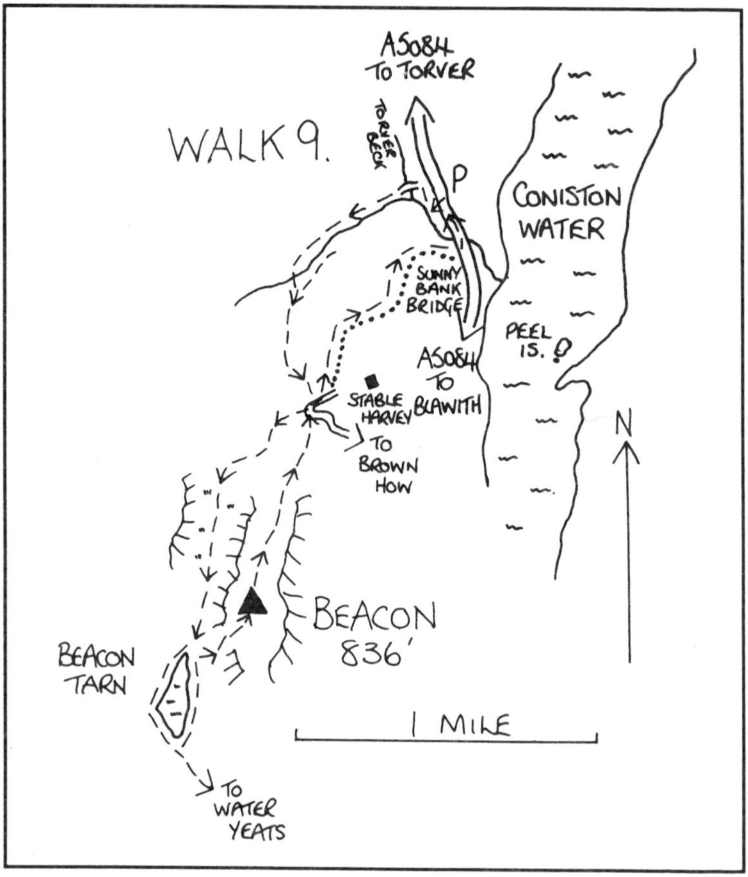

join this but first your path bears right, crossing a deeply cut stream. If you look back to your right around here you will get an impressive view of the Coniston Fells. Wetherlam is on the right, leftwards rise Coniston Old Man, Dow Crag, Walna Scar and the pointed peak of Caw.

The path begins to bear left, first crossing Meres Beck, then a boggy section and a shallower stream, to join with the path previously mentioned. This path now bears left around a hill to emerge above a hollow with two isolated trees in its bottom and walls above to the left. Beyond the hollow, Beacon rises impressively and now an obvious path can be seen slanting up to the gap mentioned. To reach this path drop down into the hollow and up the other side to meet a tarmac road. Turn right down this until it begins to swing left where a path can be seen continuing straight ahead. Follow this path over two hummocks, under power lines, and over a stream by stepping stones. It then goes left around the base of a hillock and then around a bog. Follow it, left, across a shallow stream and around a rocky rib to meet another path. Turn right along this which bears left around another bog. When it forks follow the upper path which slants rightwards, through the bracken, to reach the gap. The view of the Coniston Fells has now opened up to include the Yewdale Fells, with the Fairfield Fells beyond.

The gap turns out to be a sloping shallow valley and the path keeps to its left-hand side under the heathery, rock-scattered slopes of Beacon. The ground levels off into a boggy area with ponds, keep to the left. Then it climbs again to reach a saddle from which Beacon Tarn can be seen below. Follow the path down to the tarn. All this is National Trust land and you may wander at will. To climb Beacon continue along the left-hand side of the tarn for a short way until a grassy opening appears in the heather to your left. Climb up this to find a path slanting left up into the heather, with rocks on its right. When the angle eases the path bears right towards a cairn in the heather. it begins to climb again then eases and bears right to where other paths come in from the right. The path now swings left and climbs up to the left of a rocky hummock. It becomes stony and bears right, up the face of the hummock. You are now on the summit ridge and the cairn is a short way ahead.

Just before reaching it a superb view of Coniston Water suddenly opens up before you. The little island off the wooded promontory is Peel Island, the 'Wild Cat Island' of Arthur Ransome's famous book *Swallows and Amazons.* The Coniston Fells command the head of the lake and beyond them can be seen the Fairfield and High Street Fells. Looking back gives a view of Black Combe and to the left of that the waters of Morecambe Bay.

For the descent go past the cairn, in the direction of Coniston, keeping to the left of the crest. Continue down the path slightly below and to the left of the crest which leads into a rocky chute with a smooth slab on your left. Soon a path will be seen dropping down into a boggy hollow on the left. Follow this to cross a small stream. Continue left, around another boggy hollow, before dropping right again. A good general guide is to head down towards the tarmac road or towards the farm on the hill ahead. The path now bears left across a stream before going down and over a hummock, below power lines. Beyond this a stream is crossed to reach the road. Turn left along the road and follow it around to a gate. To the left of the gate is a sign 'Sunnybank'. Turn left and follow the wall. Stay with the wall over the hill and down through junipers to reach the road just to the right of Sunny Bank Bridge. Turn left over the bridge and back up to the car park.

Walk 10 **Medium Walk, 4-5 miles**

The Park

A short but interesting walk, the first half being through woodland, the second across open moorland, with excellent views down onto Coniston Water and across to the Coniston Fells. The first section is boggy in places and the moorland could be awkward in mist as the path is indistinct. Worth leaving for a fine day for the views. All the climbing is in the first mile or so.

Parking: From Coniston or Hawkshead follow the road along the eastern shore of Coniston Water, south past Brantwood, to park in the Beck Leven Forestry Commission car park (GR:311952).

LEAVE the car park, go back to the road and turn left. After about four hundred yards walking you will see a footpath sign 'Hawkshead'. Follow this. The path climbs up through the woods to reach a stile and gate. Cross the stile and continue upwards through birch, alder and ash, and over outcroppings of Silurian rock, to pass to the right of a stone building. Beyond the building the angle eases and a glimpse may be had through the trees on your left of the Coniston Fells. After passing through a grove of larches the path crosses a stream and divides, one fork climbing uphill and bearing right, the other turning left alongside the stream. Turn left and follow the stream which is soon joined by another stream coming in from the right. Turn right along this stream. The path is virtually in the bed of this stream for a short way before emerging on the opposite bank. The path climbs, bearing right, then passes between old gateposts before leading into a straight grassy glade between spruces. The glade is partially blocked in places by fallen trees. Soon a pile of stones is passed, a stream crossed and a stile reached. Cross the stile and continue to a further stile. Soon you will see the roof of buildings (Lawson Park) above and to your left beyond a deep stream bed. Cross another stile. Around here you will catch a glimpse of the Coniston Fells behind you. Soon yet another stile is reached which leads onto a forest road. Turn right along this for a short way until another road is met branching-off to the left. Follow this.

This road climbs across an area of open ground and there is a superb view to your right of Coniston Water and the fells beyond. The road soon enters woodland again. Shortly it joins another road at a T-junction. Turn left here. The road now climbs and curves up to another T-junction. Turn right here. After a short way the road turns sharply left. You leave it here and continue straight ahead into a gap between trees. The way is very boggy at first but soon a path becomes defined. The path eventually emerges into a cleared area. Keep to the bottom

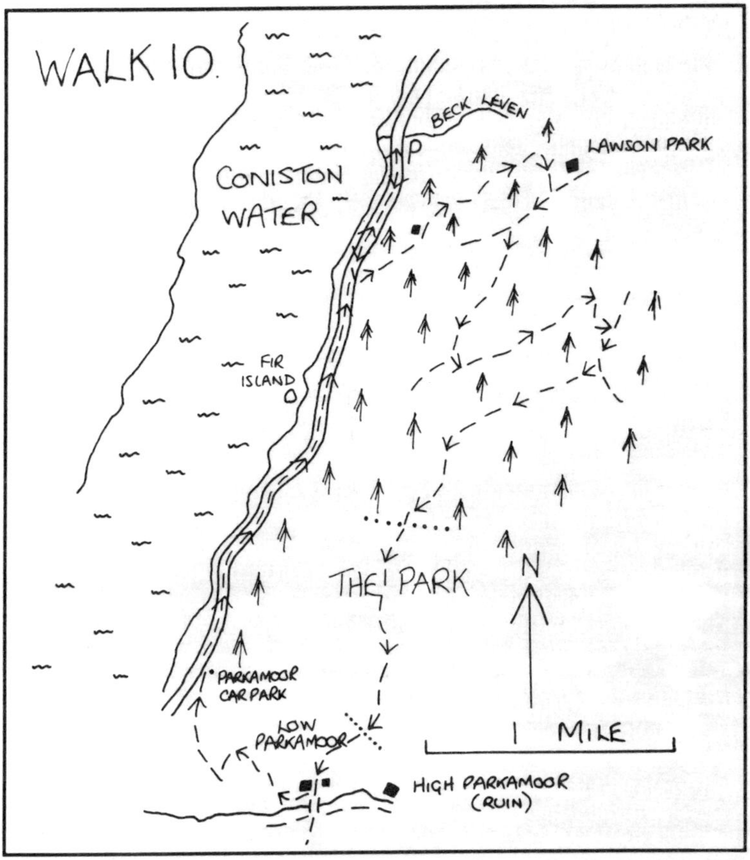

of this and along the edge of the wood and into the gap beyond. At a point where Land Rover tracks swing left, ignore them and follow the original path down into a dip rightwards. The path climbs to the left out of the dip and becomes rocky for a short way before becoming somewhat wet again. Eventually it emerges from the trees onto an open moor (The Park). Walk a few yards to your right to the edge of the escarpment for a fine view down onto Coniston Water and across to Beacon, with Black Combe beyond and to its right.

The path across The Park is indistinct, so simply head towards the obvious enclosed fields in the hollow ahead. Before reaching the first wall you should meet a path which leads through an open gate and down to and between abandoned farm buildings. Depending upon the map you are using these buildings will be labelled either Low Parkmoor or Spy Hill.

Pass between the buildings and go down between walls towards a bridge over a stream. Before reaching this, however, look for a gap in the wall to your right and an obvious green path leading from it and around and down the fellside to the right. Follow this path which leads down into woods in delightful zig-zags eventually to reach the Parkmoor car park. Turn right here and follow the road back to your car. I try to cut down road-walking to the minimum but this road is reasonably quiet even in summer and the views across the lake are delightful.

Walk 11 **Medium Walk, 8 miles**

Claife Heights

An enjoyable, nowhere strenuous, but oft-times boggy walk, through a mixture of woodland and open ground. The terrain gives varied views, highspots being the view from Wise Een Tarn of the Langdale Pikes and the 'bird's-eye' view on to Bell Isle and Bowness from Claife Heights. Bonuses are a chance of spotting deer, woodland birds, and wild fowl on the many tarns, named and un-named.

Parking: Hawkshead car park.

WALK back out of the car park and turn right. Turn left at the T-junction in the direction of 'Far Sawrey/Ferry'. Turn left again at the signpost 'Wray/Wray Castle'. Turn left at the next junction and walk through the hamlet of Colthouse, formerly a Quaker settlement. Follow the road up the hill to a gate on your right, opposite a drive entrance, signposted 'Public Bridleway — Claife Heights'.

Go through the gate and climb the worn path, alongside a fence, with a glimpse to your right of the Coniston Fells rising beyond Hawkshead. Climb further and Esthwaite Water will be glimpsed below. After passing a tarn in the woods to your right the trees and walls gradually close in before a gate is reached. (A roe deer once allowed itself to get trapped between me and this gate before bolting past me and down the path.)

Beyond the gate a sign on your right indicates 'Ferry/Sawrey' straight ahead. Descend to a forest road, where a 'Ferry' sign directs you to the right. The road descends then climbs left. As you crest the hill the road ahead can be seen to climb right. Follow it by all means, but a

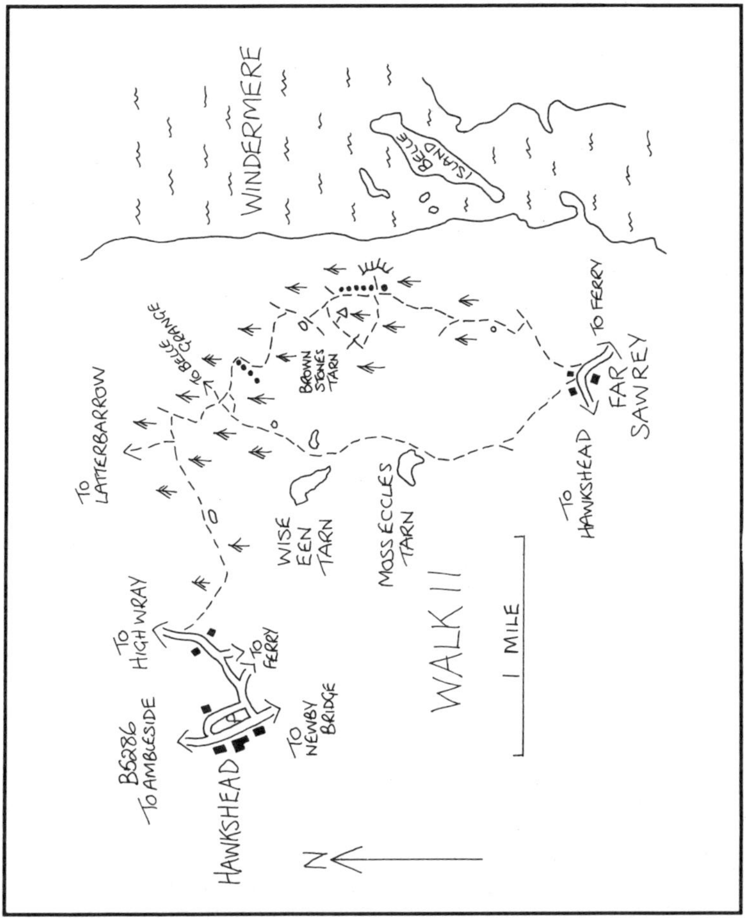

path climbing right hereabouts, between trees and a fence, provides a short cut, emerging onto the forest road above the bend. The road narrows into a path which passes to the right of a reedy un-named tarn. Pass through a waymarked gate and follow a wall onto open ground overlooking an un-named tarn on your left and larger Wise Een Tarn, 'tarn among the willow trees', to your right. North-westerly, and far beyond the glimmering waters of Wise Een, rise Bowfell's dark pyramid and the rugged, well-known outlines of the Langdale Pikes. The path passes below the dam of the smaller tarn, climbs over a rise, then drops down beside the rock-girt waters of Moss Eccles Tarn. A gate leads into a walled lane. Some distance down it look for a fork left, signposted 'Far Sawrey'. Descend to a footbridge over a beck, then join a tarmac drive and turn right eventually to emerge onto the B5285 in the hamlet of Far Sawrey, 'a muddy place'.

Turn left, passing the Sawrey Hotel, then turn left again, just past a telephone box, along a path signposted 'Public Bridleway/Claife Heights'. This path eventually climbs right over a rise, passes through a gate and turns left up a walled path signposted 'Hawkshead'. At the top bear right, past a tiny tarn, before climbing between woods into an open area where the path forks. Descend right, following the 'Hawkshead' sign on the wall to your right. Soon the path climbs steeply up Low Pate Crag. Catch a glimpse of Windermere over your right shoulder. When the angle eases and the dark conifers close in look for a path leading through a gap in the wall to your right. Follow it on to a rocky ridge giving a superb 'bird's-eye' view of Belle isle and Bowness. Return through the gap and turn right, shortly to reach a path fork with a 'Hawkshead' sign and white arrow pointing left. Climb left, following white marker posts, to reach the rock-crowned summit of High Pate Crag. Here, a 'Hawkshead' sign directs you right down a conifer tunnel, followed by a climb on to another rocky outcrop. Here, another 'Hawkshead' sign points you right down to a footbridge over a beck. Follow marker posts in a further climb to where a 'Viewpoint' sign directs you right on to the rocky summit of High Blind How. Return to the path and turn right, down on to a crossing path.

Variation: (This point can be reached more directly, should you wish to avoid the climbing, by going to the right of the 'Hawkshead' sign and white arrow, along a boggy path to the left of an old wall. Shortly after passing the opening of a conifer tunnel forking right you meet the white-waymarked path descending from High Blind How.)

Turn left and follow the marker posts to emerge on to a forest road. Turn right, signposted 'Hawkshead', and shortly pass a sign indicating 'Brown Stones Tarn' to your left. Shortly beyond this a 'Hawkshead' sign directs you left into the woods. White marker posts and waymarked rocks lead you through conifer aisles and tunnels. Soon after an old wall is seen in the trees to your left, a cairn and 'Hawkshead' sign, near a clearing, indicate a left turn. Go left eventually to emerge on to the bend of a forest road. Walk straight ahead along the road to rejoin your outward route where you took a 'short cut' right.

Walk 12 **Medium Walk, 5-6 miles**

A Grizedale Forest Walk

The tiny hamlet of Grizedale lies in the centre of the Grizedale Forest. It includes the famed Theatre in the Forest, a Wildlife and Visitor Centre, and from it spreads a delightful network of forest walks, details of which can be obtained from the Information Office. Before you embark on the walk described below, it would be useful to obtain the pamphlet describing the numbered 'points of natural history' that are passed en route.

Parking: As you approach from Hawkshead, drive past the Visitor Centre and turn left between high stone gateposts to park in the grounds of Grizedale Hall. (GR:336943)

WALK back through the gateway and turn right, along the road and past a house, then right on to a path signposted 'Silurian Way'. Climb the path, keeping your eyes open for a reptilian-looking sculpture in a hollow to your right. There are many bizarre 'sculptures' spread throughout the Forest. Continue climbing, ignoring a 'Public Footpath' sign pointing to a gate on your right. Eventually the angle eases, the walls on either side fall away, and after passing a dinosaur-like creation on your right you join a forest road or 'cycle-way'.

Turn right and follow this, shortly to descend to a T-junction with another forest road. Turn left alongside a high fence surrounding some reedy ponds. A 'hide' will be seen in the trees crowning the bank ahead and to your right. At the brow of the hill look left for a glimpse of the fells forming the famous Fairfield Horseshoe walk. Bear right, following the green waymarkers along the forest road, which twists and undulates before descending, bearing left around outcrops of rock. A swing right at the foot of the hill brings you to a 'Grizedale Tarn' signpost. Walk left through the trees on to the tiny wooden jetty overlooking this dark conifer-shadowed water. Return to the forest road and turn left to a T-junction. Turn left, following the green waymarkers. Ignore a left fork, when you reach it, and continue through an area unpleasant at the time of writing due to tree-felling. Eventually things improve and an area of mixed woodland, a pleasant change from the sombre conifers, is passed through with the ground falling away to your left. Look out for a small wooden shelter on the bank to your right, with a picnic table and benches further left, a pleasant spot for lunch whilst gazing south for a distant glimmer of Morecambe Bay.

Continue down the forest road to where a path forks right alongside an old wall, indicated by a red-topped signpost with an 'S' carved in it. Ignore this and continue down the forest road to where another path

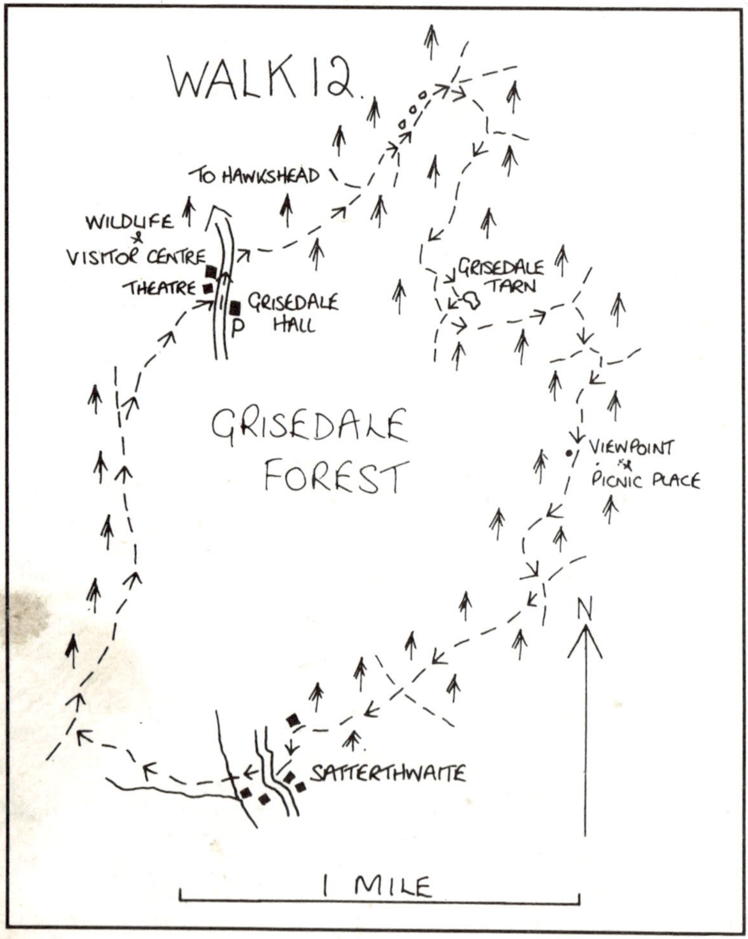

forks right, indicated by a blue-arrow on a yellow background waymarker, and blue marker posts. Turn right and follow this through the woods, alongside an old wall at times, to emerge on to a forest road. Cross this and go into the woods again down a blue-waymarked path, eventually to emerge on to a tarmac lane. Turn left and follow this down into the hamlet of Satterthwaite.

Satterthwaite means 'clearing of the summer pastures', whilst Grizedale means 'valley of the pigs'. Both have their roots in the influx of Norsemen into Cumbria in the tenth century. These 'invaders' were political refugees from Norse settlements in Ireland rather than the oft-portrayed bloodthirsty and pillaging Vikings. For your interest, and spiritual and temporal well-being, Satterthwaite contains both a church and a pub.

In Satterthwaite turn right then almost immediately left along a path signposted 'Public Bridleway/Coniston'. Follow the path past a play area, then alongside Farra Grain Gill. When the path climbs right to a T-junction with a forest road, turn right. Eventually this road forks. Take the right fork, across a cattle grid, and follow it down into Grizedale.

Walk 13 **Medium Walk, 5 miles**

Goosey Foot Tarn and Hawkshead Moor

An easy and delightful walk combining the pleasures of woodland and open fellside and giving some superb views of the fells of Eastern Lakeland and the Pennines, ranging from Ingleborough to Helvellyn.

Parking: Hawkshead village car park.

LEAVE the car park and go past the toilets onto the main street and turn right, towards the church. In the square below the church, find and climb the steps leading up into the churchyard. Follow the path through the gravestones around to the west end of the church to where a path leads up to an iron-gate. Go through this and follow the path leading between gravestones on the left and slate-fence to the right. Look to your right to see, beyond the village, a superb view of the Eastern Fells. From right to left range Ill Bell, Froswick, Thornthwaite Crag, John Bell's Banner, with Wansfell below it, followed by the gap of Kirkstone Pass, then Red Screes, Little Hart Crag, Dove Crag, Hart Crag and Fairfield.

Eventually a wooden gate is reached and passed through to find a footpath sign in the field beyond. Follow the right-hand pointer 'Tarn Hows/Coniston' across the field to a gate leading into a lane. Go along the lane to a T-junction with a further lane. Turn left here and follow the path leading uphill, past Owl House, ignoring the gate and footpath sign on your right. Continue to climb, with a stream and cascades to your left. The path eases, to cross a branching stream, before climbing again to a gate. Beyond the gate the path bears left, crosses a stream, then follows a wall. Beyond the wall can be seen the wooded hills of Furness and far beyond them the hump of Ingleborough.

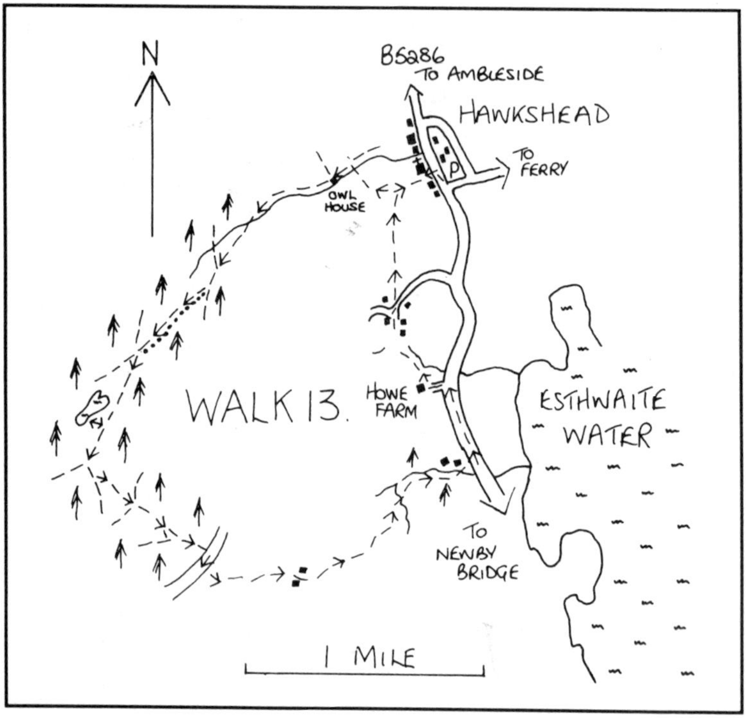

A glimpse of Esthwaite Water may also be seen down to the left. Soon a forest road is met. Turn left along this. After a short way a footpath, running alongside an old wall, will be seen on your right. Follow this; it leads to a function of forest roads. Turn left here.

Shortly you will see a tarn through the trees on your right and soon you will reach a path leading towards it. This is Goosey Foot Tarn. The Forestry Commission in co-operation with the Wildfowlers' Association are using this area for a wildfowl project for the re-establishment of greylag geese. Return to the forest road and continue along it until a T-junction with another forest road is reached. Turn left here and then almost immediately left again down a path. This path descends to merge with forest roads coming in from right and left. Continue on until a short branch road will be seen on the right leading down to a lower forest road. Around here make a detour left to climb to the crest of a cleared ridge to see a superb view that runs from Ingleborough, to the far right, to Nethermost Pike on Helvellyn, to the extreme left. The lower wooded hills almost immediately across the valley are Claife Heights, with the rounded bare summit of Latterbarrow at their left-hand end. The distant, gracefully sculpted, hills above and beyond them are the Howgills, above Sedbergh. To the left of Latterbarrow a glimpse of Windermere can be seen.

Return to the forest road and continue along it until another forest road joins from your right. Continue on to cross a cattle-grid and reach the Hawkshead to Grisedale road. Turn right up this to reach a footpath sign 'Hawkshead Field/High barn'. Turn left here and follow the path wending down through junipers to reach the farm of High Barn. Go through the gate, then between buildings to a further gate. Pass through this to by-pass a third gate by a stile. A boggy and indistinct path now bears left, at a yellow-waymarker, to follow an old hedge line. Soon another waymarker will be seen, above a hollow. A faint path slants to the left down into the hollow then bears right, at another waymarker, to follow a fence and wall downhill. Look for another waymarker through a gap in the wall, to your left. Go through the gap and follow a path running to the left around a hillside, with a view of Esthwaite Water below. At an oak tree and another waymarker the path heads downhill towards an iron gate in the bottom corner of the field, beyond a waymarker and stream.

Pass to the right of the waymarker, cross the stream and climb up to the gate. Beyond the gate a track leads downhill, with a ravine to its left, to a hamlet. Cross the stream and pass between the houses to reach the road. Turn left here. Soon a lane, signposted 'Howe Farm', will be seen on your left. Climb this until just before the farm you see a sign 'Hawkshead/Roger Ground'. Turn right through a gate and go behind the buildings to pass through another gate. Turn right beyond this and follow first a wall and then a fence, with caravans and a stream beyond it, to reach a white iron gate in a corner. Pass through the gate and cross a bridge over a stream to follow a drive up to the left of a house. This leads between houses to meet a road. Turn right down this until a narrow lane is seen leading off to the left, indicated by footpath sign 'Hawkshead'. Follow this path which leads pleasantly back, through several gates, to a junction with the outgoing path behind Hawkshead church.

Valley Walks

Walk 14 **Valley Walk, 8 miles**

Coniston Lakeshore, Torver and Walna Scar

This walk contrasts the sylvan beauty of the lakeshore with the rugged splendour of the high fells. Yet throughout it there is evidence of man's restless, ingenious energy, from sites of lake-shore bloomeries to the brooding chasms of Banishead Quarries.

Parking: Coniston village car park.

LEAVE the village by the lane leading to the steamer landing stage. Where the lane bends left a footpath sign 'Coniston Hall', will be seen on the right. Cross the stile and, turning right, follow the hedgeline and yellow waymarkers to a gate in the corner of the field. Bear right through the gate. Beyond the hedge to the left will be seen the high chimneys of Coniston Hall. Soon the hedge falls back and you will come to a junction of paths in the middle of the field. Turn left and follow the path heading towards the hall. Pass in front and to the right of the building, towards a caravan site. This Elizabethan manor-house was, in the 16th and 17th centuries, the home of the Lakeland family of Fleming but there was doubtless a dwelling-place on this site for many centuries before then.

As the path swings to the left a sign in a tree to the right indicates 'Public Footpath to Torver 2 1/2 miles'. Follow the path through the campsite, bearing left, to reach the lake-shore. Across the lake the large white building is Brantwood, once the home of the artist and writer John Ruskin. Looking back towards Coniston from around this point there is a fine view of the fells with the rugged Yewdale Fells being particularly impressive. Beyond some boat-sheds the path eventually plunges into woods and for the next two miles or so twists and turns delightfully above the clear water of the lake. You will come across many tiny, shingly beaches, ideal for picnics and bathing. Care must be taken, however, for the shores shelves drop steeply to dangerous depths. I understand that if you know what to look for, there is evidence of several 'bloomeries' along the lake-shore. These are the sites where iron was smelted in medieval times.

Eventually a wall is met, with a boathouse beyond it. Turn right

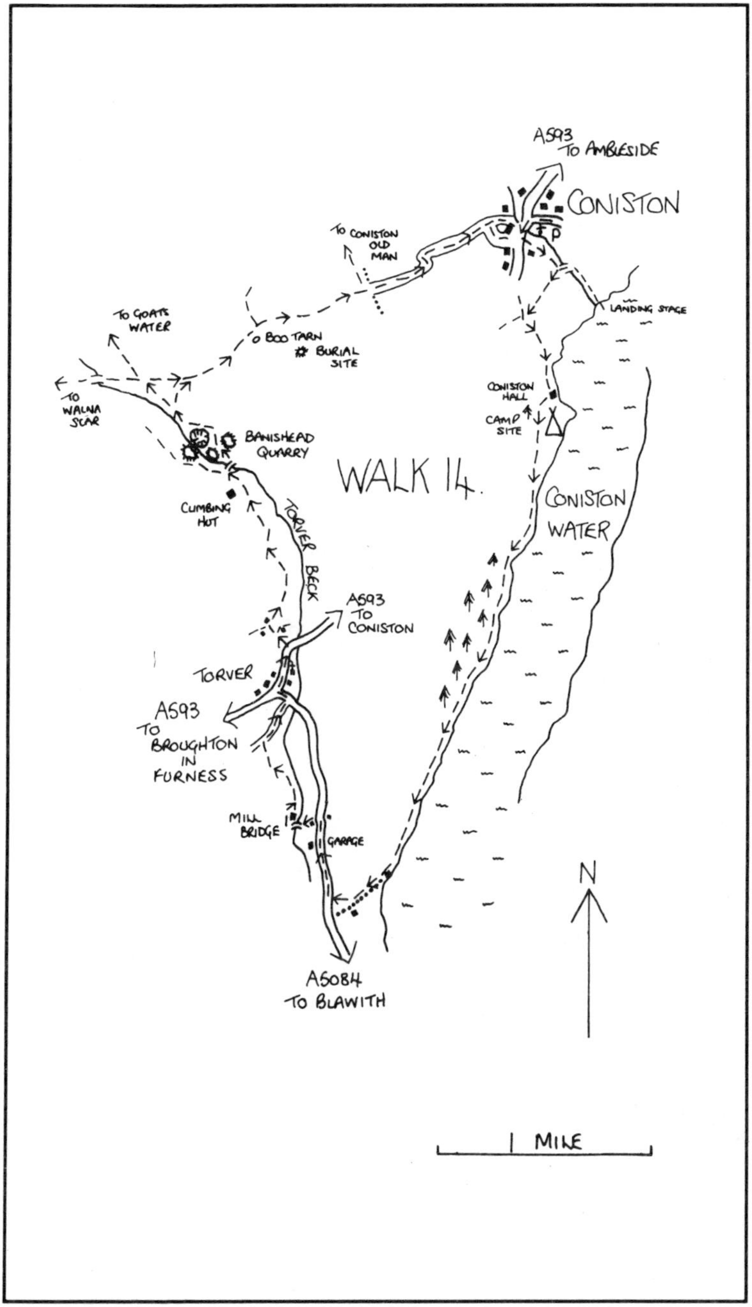
A593
TO AMBLESIDE
CONISTON
TO CONISTON OLD MAN
LANDING STAGE
TO GOATS WATER
BOO TARN
BURIAL SITE
TO WALNA SCAR
CONISTON HALL
CAMP SITE
BANISHEAD QUARRY
WALK 14.
CLIMBING HUT
TORVER BECK
CONISTON WATER
A593
TO CONISTON
TORVER
A593
TO BROUGHTON IN FURNESS
MILL BRIDGE
GARAGE
N
A5084
TO BLAWITH
1 MILE

here and follow a path running up alongside the wall to met a fence. Turn right here to meet a gate which leads onto the A5084 Coniston-Ulverston road at the Torver Common car park. (The start of Walk 9). Turn right up the road, which climbs to pass a garage. Just beyond the garage an overgrown bridleway leads down to your left. Follow this down to a bridge. As you descend a water-wheel will be seen in the stream to your right and above it a fine waterfall. Cross the bridge and pass in front of the old water-mill and around to the right to a gate above it. Pass through this and the gate beyond. The right wall drops away now and a splendid view of Dow Crag and Coniston Old Man opens up ahead. The path, a raised platform bordered by tree-stumps, follows the hedge round to a gate leading into a lane. Turn right along the lane and right again to reach the A5084 again near Torver village. Turn left here, and almost immediately right to walk through the village, passing a pub and the church. (There is a bus-service to Coniston if you feel you have walked far enough.)

Beyond the church, where the road swings right over a bridge, a lane fingerposted 'Walna Scar' climbs left. Follow this twisting lane, ignoring all openings to left or right. Eventually the tarmac ends and the track steepens and becomes stony underfoot. After passing through a gate near a ruin the left wall turns away and shortly, beyond a small quarry, a splendid view opens up ahead of Dow Crag and Coniston Old Man. Cross Tranearth Beck below the Lancashire Caving and Climbing Club Hut and continue along a stony lumpy path towards the spoil heaps of Banishead Quarry. Pass through a gate and turn right through a narrow passageway (signposted), to the right of a second gate, to cross a bridge over the Torver Beck. Climb the path through the spoil heaps to swing around to the right of a spectacular fenced-off flooded quarry with a beck cascading over its far rim. Continue up the path alongside the Torver Beck until a green path forks right. Turn right along this to shortly join the wider and stonier Walna Scar Road. Turn right along this track and just before a newish quarry road joins from the left look to your right for the small reedy depression grandiloquently christened Boo Tarn. Some 250 yards south-east, marked 'enclosure' on the 2 1/2" map, is where several Bronze Age burial urns were unearthed in 1909. Along with the ashes of a child of around three years old was a charred fragment of cloth that was one of the earliest examples of woven British cloth. The urns are now in the Ruskin Museum in Coniston.

Return to the track and follow it down to the tarmac road and so back to Coniston.

Blelham Tarn, Windermere and Latterbarrow

A splendid walk through a variety of scenery. Lunch can be taken on the shore of Windermere, and the climax of the walk, the short climb up Latterbarrow, brings you one of the finest views in Lakeland.

Parking: Hawkshead village car park.

LEAVE the car park and turn left along the road. When the road swings left look for a lane, to the left of a high wall, over the road to your right. Go down this to see a 'Footpath' sign ahead. Follow the tarmac right, then left, around a white house where it ends. A path now continues ahead to reach a footbridge over a stream. Cross this and turn left to follow the stream for a short while before bearing right to a gate. Beyond this the path slants across a field to a stile. Beyond the stile the path forks, near a large boulder. Turn left to reach another stile at the end of a wall. The path now bears slightly right, with a barn above and to your right. To your left Coniston Old Man and Wetherlam can be seen rising above the lesser fells. A gate now leads into a narrow lane; turn left up this. Soon a stile will be seen on your right below a massive oak. Cross this and follow the path climbing up beside a fence. A further stile is crossed to reach the crest of the hill. A farm will be seen ahead and to your left. Beyond this rises the rounded shape of Red Screes, above Ambleside, with John Bell's Banner to its right and the Fairfield Fells to its left.

Cross the stile ahead and follow the path to the left of a hillock to reach a road. Beyond the far wall Ambleside and the head of Windermere can be seen. Turn left between farm buildings and look for a gate on your right marked 'Footpath'. Pass through this and between walls to find a stile on your left. Ignore this and go through the gate ahead and follow the left-hand hedge to a gate and stile in the corner of the field below. Follow the path ahead over a rise with the distant and graceful shapes of Froswick and Ill Bell beyond. The path is indistinct. Follow a line of trees, which appears to be an old hedge-line, towards a pair of old gateposts in the middle of a field. Continue in the same direction, at first downhill to cross a culvert, then up to a stile in the corner of the field. Cross this and follow a faint path uphill to pass through another tree line to meet a yellow stone marker in the ground. Continue beyond this to meet a wall. Turn left now and follow the wall to meet a gate and signposts in a corner.

Ahead you will now catch a glimpse of Blelham Tarn. Any strange objects seen on its surface are part of experiments conducted by the Freshwater Biological Association. Go through the gate and head downhill to a stile/gate in corner of field. This leads onto a farm lane; turn right and up to a road. Turn left here and follow the road down until it swings right. A signpost 'Wray Castle 1 mile' will be seen on your left directing you onto a path passing in front of a farmhouse. Beyond the house a stile is crossed and the path follows a wall and fence, crosses a stream, bears left, and when Blelham Tarn is seen again, begins to bear right. Beyond Blelham Tarn you are looking straight into the heart of the Fairfield Horseshoe, a classic fell-walk. Another stile is crossed before the path drops down towards woods. Soon a finger-post directs you to the left to a gate between slate slabs. The path now swings right, around the base of a sloping field, to another gate. Follow the path towards a mound crowned by trees. Go to the left of this mound and into trees to meet a gate and a slate foot bridge over a stream. Beyond the bridge head uphill with the fence/hedge to your right. Just after passing a gate in this fence the faint path heads into a wooded dip and swings round to the right to reach a gate leading onto a road.

Turn left here and follow the road uphill to reach a church and the entrance to Wray Castle. A path to the right of the church is signposted 'Public Bridleway'. Follow this down until you see a stile on your left. This leads onto the grassy shores of Windermere — a pleasant spot for lunch. After lunch return over the stile and continue along the lane until just beyond a boathouse and a stile another stile will be seen to your right. Cross this and follow the path uphill with a wall to your right. Pass between slate gate-posts and continue uphill. A look back across the lake sees the summit of Ill Bell to the right of Wansfell, and a glance over the wall to your right gives a fine view of the Langdale Pikes. Keeping the wall on your right brings you to a gate. Continue to follow the right wall, behind a house, to reach a stile in a corner which leads onto a drive. Turn right, through a gate, and onto a road. Turn left and walk up through the hamlet of High Wray. Pass a minor road on the left marked 'Ferry — Unit for Cars' and continue uphill until a sign 'National Trust, Base Camp' points across a cattle-grid to your left.

Cross the cattle-grid and follow a rough road to a junction at a National Trust sign 'Base Camp'. The left fork leads towards buildings in the woods. You take the right fork to a gate/stile. Beyond this the road begins to swing left, uphill. Look for a path here leading to the right to a stile in a fence in the trees. This path eventually crosses a stream, follows a fence for a while, then climbs upwards through the woods, eventually emerging into a more open area to reach a stile over a wall. Beyond this a further climb brings you to the summit of Latterbarrow and a superb view. The fells seen, both high and low, are too numerous to describe. The summit of Latterbarrow is a grand spot for the knowledgeable to air their knowledge and the less

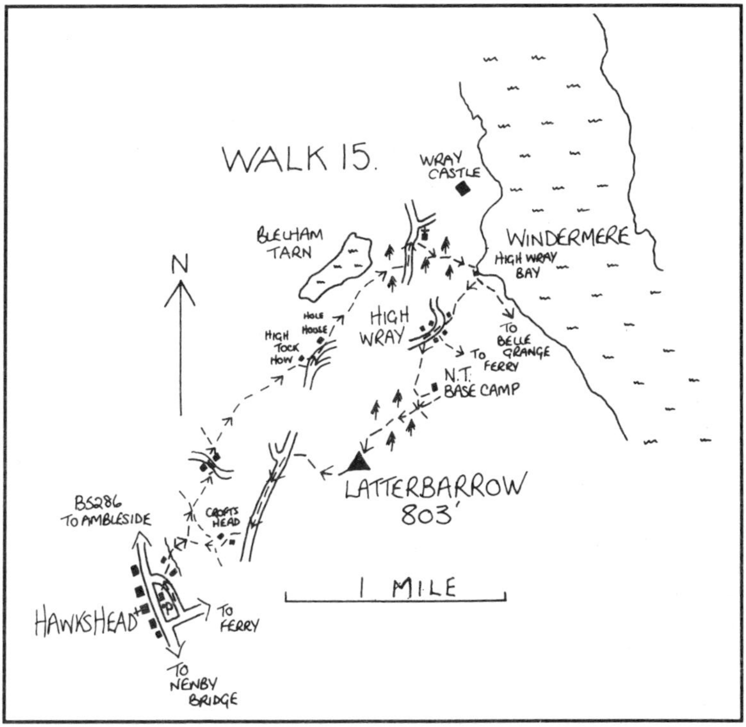

knowledgeable to get out their maps and attempt to orientate themselves.

For the descent head down in the general direction of Hawkshead (westerly). At the foot of the hill a path will be met which heads down to the right to a gate leading onto a road. Turn left down the road shortly passing another road on your right. Further down the road a lane runs down to your right towards houses. Follow this. Look for a gate to the right of a garage in an opening on your left. Go through this and follow the path, bearing right, to a slate stile. Turn left beyond this and go past a forked ash tree. Esthwaite Water may be seen to your left here. The path now goes between rock outcrops before swinging right to another stile. Beyond this head downhill to a gate leading into a narrow lane. Turn right here then almost immediately left over a stile. Follow the path, bearing right around the foot of a hillock, and you will reach your outgoing route at the fork and boulder previously mentioned. Cross the stile and return by the same route.

Boulder Valley and Levers Water

An amiable walk which passes through some remarkably rugged mountain scenery to reach the shores of a lovely mountain tarn. For those interested it also provides many aspects of the industrial history of Lakeland, from the forbidding chasm of Simon's Nick to the ruined mine-buildings of Red Dell and the Coppermines Valley.

Parking: Coniston village car park.

FOLLOW the directions given in Walk 1 as far as the bridge over Church Beck. You now cross this bridge and follow the path slanting up the fellside to your right. You have a fine view of the Coppermines Valley, with its spoil heap, ruined mine-workings, miners cottages (now holiday homes) and white-walled Youth Hostel. Above it more mine buildings guard the entrance to Red Dell, Wetherlam's high valley. Your path eventually meets a rough road. Turn right along this. It is Alpine in character with steep crags above to the left and the depths of Coppermines Valley below and to the right. The road ends abruptly but a path continues on heading towards a huge boulder perched on the edge of Low Water Beck. You are now in Boulder Valley and the huge monolith apart (known as the Pudding Stone), it is easy to see why the area got its name. The Pudding Stone can be climbed quite easily from the rear. Curving around and above the valley are the rocky ramparts of Coniston Old Man and Brim Fell, split in the middle by the splendid cascades of Low Water Beck. These spill over the lip of the corrie containing Low Water, above which the summit ridge rears against the sky. To the right of the cascades the rugged bastion of Raven Tor thrusts out from the summit of Brim Fell.

Cross the footbridge and follow the path up a grassy ridge to reach the saddle at the foot of Raven Tor. From this saddle Levers Water can be seen below. Hereabouts are several fenced-off mine shafts and on a cold day warm air can be seen venting from the bowels of the earth. Down to the right is Simon's Nick, reputedly a thousand feet deep. Examine these shafts at a distance: **they are extremely dangerous.** Go down to the dam and walk along it to the far end. The view from the dam and its virtues as a picnic and bathing spot are extolled in Walk 1. The easiest descent is to cross the outlet from the tarn, if conditions allow, and turn right down the Land Rover track on the far side of Levers Water Beck. A more interesting way, however, is to leave the dam at a point where its rear wall meets the rocks and

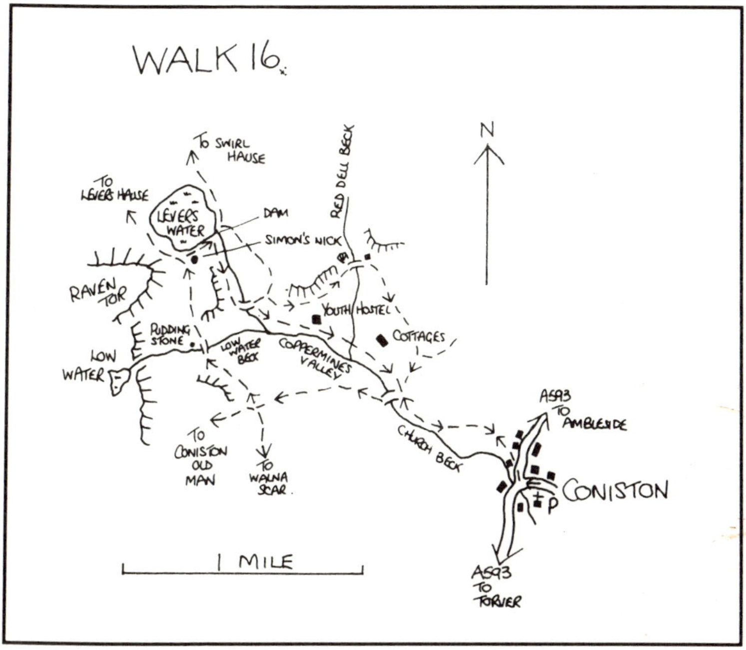

follow the path down the right-hand bank of the beck. This slants across the spoil heaps below the grim portal of Simon's Nick, with fine views of the waterfalls of the beck, to reach a footbridge at its foot. Cross the bridge to meet the Land Rover track. Turn right to follow the rough road back down to Coppermines Valley and so back to Coniston. Soon after crossing the footbridge and following the road downhill a green miners' track will be seen branching off to your left. This provides an interesting alternative to the rough road. This path contours around Tongue Brow before swinging left along the rim of a culvert cut by the miners to cross Red Dell Beck just below the impressive mine-buildings guarding the entrance to Red Dell. (If you wish to have a closer look you will find a large tunnel to the right of the building and a stone-lined pit that probably held a large water-wheel). The path now contours along the left wall of Coppermines Valley, above and behind the old miners' cottages, before dropping down to rejoin the rough road just beyond the cottages.